WRITING FOR BEGINNERS

STEP-BY-STEP

2 Manuscripts in 1 Book, Including: How to Write a Novel and How to Write a Screenplay

Sandy Marsh

More by Sandy Marsh

Discover all books from the Writing Best Seller Series by Sandy Marsh at:

bit.ly/sandy-marsh

Book 1: *How to Write a Novel*

Book 2: *Outlining*

Book 3: *Story Structure*

Book 4: *Plotting*

Book 5: *Character Development*

Book 6: *How to Write a Screenplay*

Themed book bundles available at discounted prices:

bit.ly/sandy-marsh

Table of Contents

HOW TO WRITE A NOVEL

STEP-BY-STEP

ESSENTIAL ROMANCE NOVEL, MYSTERY NOVEL AND FANTASY NOVEL WRITING TRICKS ANY WRITER CAN LEARN

SANDY MARSH

BOOK 1: HOW TO WRITE A NOVEL

STEP-BY-STEP

Essential Romance Novel, Mystery Novel and Fantasy Novel Writing Tricks Any Writer Can Learn

Sandy Marsh

reparation, damages, or monetary loss due to the information
herein, either directly or indirectly.

Respective authors own all copyrights not held by the
publisher.

The information herein is offered for informational purposes
solely, and is universal as so. The presentation of the information
is without contract or any type of guarantee assurance.

The trademarks that are used are without any consent, and
the publication of the trademark is without permission or backing
by the trademark owner. All trademarks and brands within this
book are for clarifying purposes only and are the owned by the
owners themselves, not affiliated with this document.

Table of Contents

Introduction

Thank you and congratulations on purchasing *"How to Write a Novel: Step-by-Step | Essential Romance Novel, Mystery Novel and Fantasy Novel Writing Tricks Any Writer Can Learn"*. As well, congratulations on deciding that you want to write a fiction novel!

The tips and tricks you will learn in this book will help walk you through the step-by-step process of writing your very own novel, while also making it extremely easy to stay committed! You will learn everything you need to know about simplifying the process and making it one that you can easily stick to so that you can create the fiction novel of your dreams, literally!

Each chapter in this book is dedicated to one part of the novel writing experience. You will begin by learning all about outlines and work your way through each step right down to finding the perfect reader to test out your new novel. By the time you're done reading this you will be completely finished writing your very own fiction novel.

This book was designed to help make the process easier while also making it an enjoyable experience. Understand that this is not necessarily a "conventional" how-to book as it will seek to both educate and inform while also making the process fun and exciting. Writing a book should never be boring or difficult - if it is, you are going about it all wrong! With the steps in this book, you will learn to bring back the passion in your writing and create the best fiction novel possible, whether this is your first time trying or you've done this before and you just need a boost to get through this particular book!

Please be sure to take your time and have fun with this book as the writing process truly is an experience to be enjoyed. Allow each section to provide you with tips and tricks to help lighten up the experience so that you can increase the entertainment you derive from the writing process so that you are left not only with an incredible novel but also with an experience worth remembering. This book can be used as many times as you require, so be sure to keep it handy for any fiction novels you may set out to write! And lastly, please enjoy!

Chapter 1: The Outline

As you may be aware, having an outline to a book is important. This provides you with an idea of where the story is going and what your "goals" for the book are. Many authors prefer to start with a strong outline that will give them direction and help them stay on track when they are working through the writing process. Having a strong outline that identifies major plot points means that you can continually work your story towards each new plot point in chronological order so that you ultimately end up at your "goal" outcome based on what you had included in your outline.

For many writers, an outline is an absolute must-have. They prefer to have an outline that will help guide them because this keeps them focused and working along a credible storyline that is intended to keep readers engaged. By having this the writer knows how to stay on point and how to structure different parts of the story to keep everything working towards the same goal. For others, having an outline feels too boxy and they feel as though their creative expression is being suffocated by the existence of the outline. If this is you, then you may want to consider scratching the outline altogether. Below we will explore different tips and ideas for each unique individual and how you can create an incredible story regardless of whether or not you choose to use an outline.

If You Love to Guide Your Focus…

If you love to have your focus guided towards a particular goal, such as the one at the end of your outline, then having an outline is a good idea for you. This will help encourage you to stay on track with your writing process and keep each unique element of the story focused towards the outcome. Having the outline helps you avoid yourself from putting unnecessary information in the plot line or otherwise over-explaining things that may not be relevant to the overall story itself.

Outlines are a great tool to help keep writers focused and guided throughout the process. Creating an outline is fairly simple, you think of where you want the characters to "start" and "end" in the story. Then, you decide what major plot points are going to get them from the start to the end. For example, you might have two characters in a romance novel that are going to start as best friends and end as lovers. Along the way, you might choose to include plot points such as them taking on a big project together and it brings them closer, but the competitiveness between them drives them apart. As they work through the competitiveness they discover that their relationship grows even stronger and when they complete the project they are feeling closer than ever before. Later they make excuses to hang out even more, and eventually, they end up falling in love. As you can see from this example, the outline included the main characters, the starting and ending points of the story, and major events that lead the two characters to the "finish line".

Once you have created your basic outline, you want to include even more information in it. This would include settings where each scene takes place, the emotions behind each experience, and anything else that would contribute to you setting the mental image for the scene itself. By identifying as many descriptive factors about each major plot point as possible you make it easier for you to know exactly where you are working towards in each part of the story. Of course, you can always choose to alter these if the writing process brings you towards a different idea or plot point, but having them identified and a rough outline created can help you stay on track and remain focused on what you want to take place within' the story.

If you are someone who tends to need tools such as outlines to help you stay focused and guide you through the process it is a good idea that you complete one before you start writing any part of your novel. Having the outline written and in front of you can help you identify what you like about the story and any issues that you may notice before you actually begin writing. This can help you finalize what your conflict will be an anchor in any specific details that you want to include in your writing so that you go into your novel with a clear plan and an idea of how you are going to achieve what you have set out to accomplish.

If You Love Creative Freedom...

If you are the type of writer who prefers to work alongside creative freedom and who feels suffocated by the idea of having a specific plan to work with there are a few things that you can do in order to exercise your creative freedom while still creating an incredible novel. Just because you don't want to have a specific plan doesn't mean that you cannot create some form of a plan that will help you stay focused and work towards some form of goal throughout your novel.

It is important to understand that even if you prefer having creative freedom, you still need to have some form of outline in place to help you organize your plot and stay focused towards a particular goal. This will help ensure that your book flows in such a way that people will read it and easily work towards the goal with you, rather than attempting to understand why there are so many different pieces of information floating around that seem irrelevant to the book itself.

The first idea you could use is to create a vague outline for your book. This would require you to create an ideal starting point and ending point for your novel, and then fill out the inside of the outline with a few different major plot points that will help guide you from point a to point b. Unlike a complete outline, you will only include enough information to give you a general idea of what you want to include in your book. Then, you can come up with the rest as you are in the process of writing your novel. This can help you with allowing you to have creative expression while also staying focused on the purpose of your novel and working towards it while successfully bringing your reader along with you. Ultimately, it prevents the buildup of irrelevant information or you involving anything that is not necessary to the novel itself.

It will, however, allow you to pick out the details and other smaller factors as you go so that you can allow the story to flow through you naturally, rather than feeling pressured to use extremely specific points in varying areas of your story, potentially taking away from the natural flow that you have created through your creative expression.

Another method you can use is called a hindsight outline. The only two things you need to identify in the beginning of creating this outline is the starting and ending points. You should always have some form of end goal when it comes to writing a novel so that you are clear on what you are writing towards and what you need to be building up to throughout the novel. However, with a hindsight outline, you do not need to include any information beyond these two points. All you have to do is ensure that you are working towards the end goal. As you write major plot points into your story, you can then write them into your outline. This may seem irrelevant, but you will soon understand that writing them down allows you to see where you have come from and where you want to go. It ensures that each part of the plot works together towards the goal and that it makes sense towards the overall story. Doing this prevents you from forgetting about plot points, including ones that may contradict previous ones, and get a general idea of the flow of your story in retrospect, rather than in advance.

Questions to Ask Yourself

The following questions are questions you should ask yourself when you are developing your outline. This will ensure that you have a strong plan for your outline and that no details are missed out on.

1. Where is my protagonist starting?

2. Where are they at in their life in the beginning of the story?

3. Where is my protagonist ending?

4. Where are they at in their life at the end of the story?

5. What major plot points are getting me to (or have gotten me to) the goal?

6. Do these plot points make sense together?

7. Is there anywhere that this outline is weak?

8. What else could I add to my outline to make a rich reading experience?

How you choose to create the outline for your story is unique to you and your writing preferences. Know that you are not required to create a detailed or complete outline before you begin writing your novel. However, having an outline is extremely important as it helps you keep major plot points in chronological order and to ensure that they flow well together. Still, if you prefer to write it out in detail ahead of time, or if you prefer to merely identify your goal and create your outline in hindsight, that is entirely up to you. You should never let creating an outline and identifying specific details of your story hold you back from writing the story in the first place. Knowing that there are options for you to help you stay focused or open up your creative freedom as much as you need to can help ensure that you are not intimidated by the very first step of writing your book. It also helps you feel confident knowing that you can stay focused and still create an incredible book, whether you do it the conventional way or not.

Chapter 2: Your Setting

Developing the setting for your story provides you with the opportunity to have an incredible amount of creative expression. This part of the book is also one of the first times that you will begin to get very descriptive about what is going to happen within' your book. Even if you have a complete outline that is quite detailed, this will be more defined than that.

Your setting is ultimately when and where your story happens. This is something that you need to identify beforehand so that you can keep this information flowing throughout the entire story. For example, you wouldn't want to begin writing a story that was set in the 1800s and then use slang or information that was only relevant to the 2000s or later. Identifying your setting and being very specific and clear on it ensures that your entire book is written with relevance to that setting. The following information will help you identify important tips and tricks that you should pay attention to when it comes to developing your setting for your novel.

If You Only Have One Location

If you are writing a book where the story will never venture away from your primary overall location, then you want to make sure that you are very clear and specific on this location. This is where your entire book is going to be written, so you want to be very descriptive of and clear on this location by knowing exactly what is relevant to it and what is true about it.

You should identify where this location is, what sets it apart from other locations, and why you are using this location. You also want to discover what the local culture is like (specific to your time frame) and any other identifying factors that you may learn about this place. The best way to do it is to research this place as though you were going to be a tourist. Make sure that you do it specific to the time frame, which you will learn more about in a moment. For the location-specific part, however, you want to identify what types of buildings exist in this place, what they were made of, what the roads looked like, what types of wildlife and plant life exists in the area, and anything else that will help you create a graphic image in someone's mind about the location you have chosen.

Once you have identified the location, create a list that involves as many relevant descriptive phrases as you can. You want to generate ideas of how you will describe the place to people throughout the book and creating these ideas beforehand will ensure that you are not at a loss for words or repeating your descriptions throughout the book. Having this list will help you create a dynamic description that truly helps bring the book to life for your readers and prevents them from becoming bored of the same descriptions being used over and over again.

If You Have Many Locations

If you have many locations you want to essentially conduct what you did for one location, only for many. This part of the process may seem fairly straightforward, so we are not going to further explore the process for identifying each unique location. However, there are other things you need to consider when you are using many locations in your book.

First, you want to decide which location is going to be "home" for your characters. This one, in addition to the one where your characters stay in for the longest period of time, should be the ones that you know about the most. You should have plenty of describing factors that help set the scene for what home is like for your characters, as well as for what their new place of residence is like. For example, you might set the scene for home as "The Rocky Mountains: a place where the air is cool and crisp, and the mountainous view is one that cannot be done justice short of seeing it yourself. The community is warm and cozy, especially in the cold winters when snow makes it difficult just to leave your front door." Whereas the new place of residence is described as "The prairies, where the wheat grows for miles and you can see the entire story of the sky as clouds dance across the wide-open view in front of you. The communities are cheerful and bright, and you feel like there is nowhere you can't go, and nothing to stop you from getting where you want to be." You want to describe both the location as previously mentioned and go into detail about the emotion behind each location and why these emotions differ for the protagonist.

Second, you want to identify the mode of travel if any will be used in the book. You also want to become as descriptive as possible when it comes to the mode of transport. Where does the character get on and off of it? What stands out about this mode of transport and how does it contribute to the overall story? Is there anything particular that the reader should know that will help them feel as though they are genuinely walking up to, entering, riding, and exiting the mode of transport that you have chosen? Describing the transport itself in advance will help when it comes to foreshadowing and other story-telling tactics during the writing process. Rather than leaving it up to surprise you can easily blend it into your story so that it flows effortlessly with everything you have already written up until that point, and afterward.

If You Are Making Up the Location

If you are writing a fantasy novel where you are going to be making the location up, it is important that you take the time to actually create a location that makes sense. The location you create needs to be consistent and should be relevant to the story you are telling. There are a few tips when it comes to making up a location that you can consider using to help you create an incredible location for your book.

First, consider basing your location off of somewhere that already exists. If there is somewhere on the globe that resembles what you want your fantasy world to look like, consider first creating a descriptive location setting for that place and then alternating parts of it to fulfill your fantasy world. This will assist you with keeping everything relevant and consistent across your world.

If you are going to be making up the world entirely then you want to take your time. Close your eyes and picture this world in your own mind, first. Then, write as many descriptive factors as you can about the appearance of this location. Ultimately, you want the reader to see exactly what you are seeing in your mind at the time.

You want to make sure that when you are introducing readers to your fantasy world that they feel as though they are mentally stepping into it. They should be able to find enough information in your novel that they can not only step into the world, but they can also interact with it. They should know what type of wildlife - if any - exists in the world. Give them an idea of what the colors are like, how the communities are built, what the buildings themselves look like, and what smells they can find floating around in the air. Give them an idea of what objects are around the setting so that they can mentally picture them and that they truly feel as though they are living in your imaginary world alongside your characters. This will provide you with a strong fantasy setting that will ensure that your book truly is a fantastic read.

If You Only Have One Time Period

When it comes to time periods you need to be very specific and careful. You want to choose one that would make sense to and be relevant to the story you are telling. You also want to ensure that you do enough research about it that you tell the story as though it truly is set in that time frame. A painful mistake that would truly detract from the value of your novel would be one where you choose a certain time frame and then include information that is completely irrelevant to that time frame. For example, if you chose to set your romance novel in the late 1900s but included technology such as cell phones or computers, it would not make sense to the story and would take away from the reading experience.

When you are setting the time frame you want to ensure that you do plenty of research about it. You also want to research your chosen location with relevance to the time frame. What did it look like during that time frame? What was the culture like? What were the people like? How did they treat each other? What was the common slang for that era? You want to be very specific on what it truly would have been like during that time frame so that you can walk your reader through it. Give them the opportunity to feel as though they have stepped into a time portal and they are being transported into that era, whether it be in the present or in the past.

If You Have Many Time Periods

When you are writing a story that has many time periods the tactics you use to develop the setting is similar to if you are writing a story that has many locations. Essentially, you want to ensure that you are effectively researching each time period so that you can provide relevant and factual information based on each time period. You really need to stay focused on the details you are providing so that your reader can easily be walked back and forth with you without finding irrelevant or false pieces of information anywhere within' the text. The more focused and factual you are, the better. When it comes to developing many time periods in a story, there is not much more required than you repeating the research processes several times over for each time period you will write about. Something you may want to add, however, is the mode of transportation being used to transport across time periods. Be sure that you create a piece of machinery and provide enough details about it that you can explain how it works and create a graphic image of it in the minds of your readers.

If You Are Making up the Time Period

If you are making up a time period in your novel, then you need to be extremely descriptive about this time period. You should identify what the time period is, and why it does not already exist. For example, maybe you are generating your own fantasy setting on an alternate planet and Earth has yet to exist therefore the time is not yet in history. Or, perhaps you are writing one in the future and the time has not happened yet, so you are creating it yourself. You need to be able to thoroughly understand *why* you are creating this new time period so that your readers understand as well.

In addition to knowing why, you also need to make up all of the important details about the time period. What is the culture like in this time period? What form of government or authority exists? What do people speak like? Are there any slang words used that your readers may not already know? What do these slang words mean? How do people treat each other? What parts of the community are different from anything we experience in our own world? What else sets this time period apart from what you are presently living or what we already know about? You want to make sure that you go into detail beforehand about creating this time period so that when it comes to the writing process you already know. Doing this will ensure that you stay consistent with your novel and that nothing is added that is then forgotten about and later contradicted. When you are making something up entirely it is important that you put the effort in towards making it truly believable for your readers. This will ensure that they are able to follow the story and that it flows well without having any contradictions, confusing pieces of information, or other additions that otherwise take away from the quality of the story itself.

Combining the Two

The setting of your story is a combination of the time period and the location. When you have completely researched or created each the location and the time period, you must then combine the two. This part of the process is simple, but it is important. You want to make sure that you identify anywhere in the combination where information might contradict itself or take away from the reading experience. For example, if you are writing a book set in the present about an Amish colony that still operates without running water or electricity, you need to identify these factors and explain the discrepancy. Making sure that your time and location mesh together seamlessly and that anything contradictory is explained will ensure that you have a strong setting for your story. This means that you will be able to easily and effortlessly guide your readers through the book without any part of it leading to them wondering what is truly going on with your story.

Questions to Ask Yourself

The following questions are questions you should ask yourself when you are developing your setting. This will ensure that you have a strong plan for your setting and that no details are missed out on.

1. What location(s) will my story take place in?

2. What is unique to this location?

3. How could I describe this location in five sentences or less?

4. When I read that description, can I truly see the location in my mind?

5. Are there any further descriptions I could use to strengthen the visual of my location?

6. What time period(s) will my story take place in?

7. What is unique to this time period?

8. How could I describe this location in five sentences or less?

9. When I read that description, can I truly feel and sense the time period in my mind?

10. Are there any further descriptions I could add to enrich the time period in my story?

11. Do my time period and location make sense together?

12. What describing factors can I use to explain any discrepancies between my location and time period, if there are any?

Chapter 3: The Point of View

The next part of writing your story requires you to consider which point of view you want to write from. As an author, you have the opportunity to decide exactly how the reader is going to learn about different elements of your story, as well as how those elements will feel to them. You can do this directly through the use of point of view and which you choose to write your story in.

There are a few different points of view that you can write from when it comes to storytelling. Each one has a unique element that allows you to elaborate on and recall experiences within' the story in a certain way. Some will limit you to only telling it from one perspective whereas others allow you to elaborate with multiple perspectives, or even to provide "outsiders" insight into different experiences. How you choose your point of view will also depend on a few things. Before you choose one, however, let's explore each unique point of view and the advantages and disadvantages it provides you with as a storyteller.

First Person

First person point of view is one of the most popular choices when it comes to writing novels. This is the point of view where the writer refers to the narrator as "I", "we", "me", "mine", "my", and "us". This is similar to if you were telling a story from your own past to someone who was standing in front of you. When you are telling a story from the first-person point of view you must pick which protagonist is going to be the storyteller in your book. Typically, it is the heroic character or the one that is involved in the majority of the scenes that will be chosen as the first-person narrator. However, you can choose virtually anyone you want, dependent upon who is going to be the best angle for you to speak from.

When you write in the first person, you provide a very natural flow to your story. Your reader will feel as though you are telling them *your* story, and if you can effectively captivate them then it will actually begin to feel like your reader is the narrator. Using "I" sentiments and first-person narrative allows your reader to fully immerse themselves in the novel and get a true, deep insight into how the narrator was feeling during each scene. You also only have to pay attention to and fully develop the mind of one character: the narrators. This is the one that you will need to have the most insight to. The rest will be based on how the narrator perceives them, which means that you don't have to go quite as deep or know every minute detail of each person. However, this can also lead to some disadvantages. For example, you are limited to only reflecting on and elaborating the story based on what the narrator would feel. You cannot explore anyone else's feelings unless you use tactics such as conversation to help the narrative character explore the feelings and thoughts of another. While this is an effective tactic, you aren't going to be able to use it in every single scene or the story will sound strange and unnatural. Furthermore, the narrative character must always be involved in or at the center of every event that takes place in the book. Otherwise, large portions are going to be missed or you are going to bounce between different points of view which is not effective.

Some ways that people have managed to use the first-person narrative while still maintaining the insights on several characters at once is by developing books whereby each chapter or section is narrated by a different character. This provides the reader with the opportunity to see into several different characters and their experiences, but it can also jolt the flow of your story and result in your readers struggling to really connect with each character the way they could if you maintained a single first-person narrative.

Second Person

Second person is an undesirable choice when it comes to writing fiction, but some people choose to use it when they are writing short stories. This is an interesting point of view to write from, but it rarely creates the ability for an author to produce an entire novel without the novel sounding strange and lacking natural flow. Second person is the "you" narrative, whereby you refer to the person reading or the narrator as "you". For example, "you were standing on a street corner when suddenly someone bumped into you." The entire book would be written in this point of view which, as you might be able to tell, is not ideal. While some books have been written this way, most publishers advise against it and will even refuse to publish books that have been written in this narrative.

The only advantage to writing in the second person narrative is that your book will be unique and eccentric. Based on the nature of this narrative you gain the ability to speak directly to the reader which can be an interesting technique, but it also does not offer you a strong advantage in storytelling. For the most part, anything written in the second person narrative that is longer than a few hundred words feels uncomfortable and sounds "off" to the reader. They will likely grow tired of the eccentric feel and simply begin feeling as though the writing is uncomfortable and strange. Furthermore, it says that you are unprofessional and are inexperienced when it comes to novels. Unless you are a highly experienced writer who has already developed a name for themselves, it is typically best that you avoid this point of view.

Third Person

Third person is the point of view whereby someone completely outside of the story is telling it. For example, using identifiers such as "he" or "she" instead of "I" or "you". This point of view is another popular one when it comes to writing fiction novels because it provides the author with the ability to provide insight into many different elements of each character. It also provides the author with a greater ability to influence the reader's emotions towards various characters without that influence being limited to what would be true and natural for any given character within' the book. For example, perhaps the protagonist hates the antagonist for something he's done wrong. In the first person, you would be required to establish feelings of hatred towards the antagonist. In the third person, however, you can further explain the situation and provide the reader with insight as to how it was a mistake and the protagonist was carrying a grudge over something that was a misunderstanding, for example. It provides you with a stronger power to shape and influence the story in a highly unique way.

When it comes to writing in the third party there are two different types you can write in: third person limited omniscience, or third person unlimited omniscience. Since each one is so unique, we are going to explore them in two different subsections below.

Before we dive in, however, please note that in the following subsections we will discuss a tool many authors use whereby they speak in the third person from a different character's point of view in each scene or chapter. This helps naturally break up the story without confusing the reader along the way. This should not be confused with the technique whereby authors write one chapter per character from the first-person point of view. Although the techniques are virtually the same, they do involve writing from a different point of view in each style.

Third Person Limited Omniscience

Third person limited omniscience means that the author has the power to enter the mind of only a few characters within' the novel. Usually, during this type of experience, the author would write from the point of view of one character per chapter or per scene to avoid confusion. When it comes to this viewpoint, the author would still write with the "he" or "she" descriptors, but would primarily focus on one character per scene or chapter.

This point of view provides the author with the opportunity to enrich the experience by providing viewpoints from many different characters, thereby giving the reader a greater amount of detail and depth into each scene and experience within' the book. It also provides the author the opportunity to write from a broader scope where they are not required to limit their story to a single person's experiences. Instead, you can elaborate on experiences that may take place without one or more of the character's present. The biggest disadvantage of this is that for the author it

requires you to take more time to make each part of the book flow
naturally, as well as to provide distinctive voices for each
character so as not to confuse yourself or your reader.
Furthermore, if you switch too often you will break up the flow of
your story and create an unnatural and uncomfortable. It is
important that you take your time and truly dedicate if you are
going to use this practice, also. Many authors find that they write
in this point of view for a few chapters and then they wind up
writing from the first-person narrative for the remainder of the
book. This laziness can result in your first chapters, or last
chapters needing to be repaired so that the entire book is written
in the same narrative and flows smoothly.

Third Person Unlimited Omniscience

Third person, unlimited omniscience is virtually the same as
limited omniscience, except that the author is not restricted to
only sharing the experience from a few character's points of
view. Instead, they can shift into the mind of any character
within' the story and provide their viewpoint on the events that
are taking place.

While this may provide the author with the opportunity to elaborate and provide great detail and depth to the story, it can also result in them getting far too carried away if they are not careful. Writing from too many different points of view can diffuse the entire story and result in the author washing out any storyline that may have taken place. It is similar to the mistake of oversharing or otherwise providing far too much information, well beyond what the reader needs to know. Although it may give them a strong understanding of each scene, it can also cause for it to take far too long to "get to the point already". It is generally advised against the idea of you writing in third person unlimited omniscience unless you are using the technique strategically to avoid damaging your storyline.

How to Choose

There is one incredibly each tactic to use when it comes to deciding which point of view you want to use when it comes to sharing your story. Consider taking one small scene from the book and then writing that scene in three different narratives: first person, third person limited omniscience, and third person unlimited omniscience. Only write a few short paragraphs in each point of view so that it doesn't take too long, but be sure that you write them well. Then, read each one. This will give you an idea as to how each point of view would shape the reader's experience and what "feel" it gives to your story. It also provides you with some practice as to how each point of view feels as the author and if it gives you the ability to express yourself in the way that you want to be expressed.

Questions to Ask Yourself

The following questions are questions you should ask yourself when you are choosing your point of view. This will ensure that you have a strong plan for your point of view and that no details are missed out on.

1. Who do I want to tell my story?

2. What feeling do I want my readers to have?

3. Which point of view is going to be reasonable for me to write an entire novel in?

4. Will this give me the opportunity to express my
    story the way I want to?

5. Is there any way that this might limit my story or
    otherwise hinder the reader's experience?

Chapter 4: Characters

Naturally, your story needs characters. After all, what story are you telling if there is no one taking part in the story itself? Creating a strong story requires for you to have strong, well-developed characters involved. If you are looking for greater insight as to how you can develop well-rounded characters I encourage you to read book 6 from this series: *"Character Development*: Step-by-Step."* Because I provide you with such great detail on how to develop your characters in that novel, I will not go into elaborate detail on character development in this chapter. Instead, we are going to identify other important information about your characters, such as who needs to be involved in the story and how they contribute. Knowing this basic information is powerful in regard to the actual writing process. This will help you when it comes to outlining and creating a plan for the direction of your story. When it comes to the actual writing process, however, you will want to make sure that you have fully developed characters so that they are realistic and can add to your story in a powerful way. In the meantime, let's explore other important aspects of characters in your story.

The Value of Your Characters

Characters are a powerful element of your story because they truly drive the story forward. Without characters, the story simply cannot move forward because there would be nothing to talk about. Your characters help you not only convey the story but also express it in certain ways. Depending on what point of view you have chosen, your characters can be used in unique ways to manipulate the reader's thoughts and feelings about other characters, as well as about the storyline and events that take place within' the story.

Think of professional dancers. Music is put on as the foundation for the story and it can be related to the setting. The words that coincide with the music, or the song lyrics, are responsible for providing you with insight into what the song is about. Once the dancers begin dancing, however, they can manipulate how you feel about the song, what emotions are provoked within' you, and how you take in the experience as a whole. Without the dancers, it would simply be a song with lyrics. With the dancers, it is a story with a soul.

The same goes with writing books. The setting is the foundation for your story, and the narrator is the one who tells the story. Your characters, however, provide the heart and soul of your story. They are the ones that you can use to help manipulate the readers' thoughts and provoke different emotions in them so that they experience the book in the way that you want them to. While each unique reader may have a slightly different experience, the overall interpretation of the book will remain fairly similar if you use your tools or characters, properly.

Choosing Your Protagonist

Because of how important characters are, it is vital that you choose a good character to be your protagonist. Your protagonist needs to be a strong character who can lead the story in a powerful way. When you are putting together the outline and idea for your story, consider which specific character would be best at bringing readers through the story in an effective manner that would allow you to create the experience you want to create. Which of your characters will be involved in the most experiences? Which ones will have the best emotional attachment to the storyline so that they can move your readers for you? If you are writing from a first-person narrative, you need to choose a single character that is going to be able to effectively move everyone through the entire novel. For example, it may be the wife, best friend, teacher, and book club host. Because this particular character is involved in so many different elements of the community she may be the best individual and voice to help you tell the story with a great level of depth and dynamic so that the reader truly has an incredible experience. If you are writing in the third party, however, make sure that you choose powerful characters that you will write from. These would-be ones that all connect in one way or another and that have stories that will link together. This ensures that each character makes sense to the narrative. If you are writing in third-party unlimited omniscience, make sure that when you move to the narrative of someone who may be new or unique to a specific part of the story that this move makes sense and it is clear to the reader as to why you are doing this. This will ensure that you are drawing the reader through a clear and logical storyline that makes sense.

How Many Characters Do You Really Need?

The number of characters you choose to have in your story is really unique to the story you are trying to tell. If you are telling a romance novel, for example, you may only have two primary characters and a handful of other characters that contribute to the story. For example, some best friends, family members, the cashier at the drug store they always stop at, or the receptionist at the hotel where they celebrate their honeymoon. When you are planning your story, you need to consider how many characters are actually going to be required in order for you to tell the story. As you carry on you may discover that you need to add more characters along the way, so it is not mandatory for you to identify every single character you are going to write about immediately. However, you should have a good idea of who your primary and secondary characters are going to be. Remember, your primary characters are the ones that show up in nearly all scenes and your secondary ones are characters that are recurring in a major way.

What Your Characters Say About Your Book

The characters you choose are going to say a lot about the book you are writing and the story you are telling. These characters have the power to shape the reader's perception of the book, as well as gain an even deeper insight as to what the setting is like and the feelings they should be deriving from the general information you are providing. For example, if you are writing a book from the late 1990's about a town in the southern states, you could write about a wealthy family or a poor family. This would shape your character's point of view on the entire setting and emotions associated with the book, as well as how they perceive your characters. It also helps round out your story. The characters you choose, how you design them, and how you portray them will all contribute to the story you tell. In the previous example, one story might provide the reader with a country glamorous feeling where they ride horses and own a large farm with stable hands, whereas the other might provide your family with a poorer country feel where they *are* the stable hands and they live in a shack built on the corner of the property. Who you choose for your characters will provide greater depth for your story and ultimately be the final factor that provides your reader with the clear picture of what they see, think, and feel as they read the story you have written for them.

Questions to Ask Yourself

The following questions are questions you should ask yourself when you are developing the basic outline for your characters. This will ensure that you have a strong plan for your character development and that no details are missed out on. Remember to check out book 6 where we go deeper into the creation and development of characters so that you have a strong selection of characters to help move your story forward.

1. What story am I telling and who is the focus of the story?

2. What point of view am I writing in and whose point of view do I want to write from?

3. What recurring characters are an important element of this story?

4. Are there any additional characters that will be
    involved in key plot points?

5. How do these specific characters help move the
    story?

Chapter 5: Conflict

Every good novel comes with a fair amount of conflict involved. If there was no conflict, then there would be nothing that really keeps the reader engaged. Everyone loves a great happy-ending story, but most like to see the work that goes into creating that happy ending. This is somewhat like providing a realistic snippet of your character's lives to your readers. No one's real life is easy all of the time, so writing an entire novel where all of your characters never experience any true conflict is not only unrealistic but also boring. It takes away from the entire reading experience by never giving any depth or diversity to your story.

Creating conflict in your novel should be an ongoing process. It is not simply about having one major conflict and everything being sunshine and rainbows up until and after that point. Instead, it is about leading up to the conflict, and about coming down from it as well. You want to have one primary conflict that drives the story, but you should include many other conflicts along the way as well. These smaller conflicts add more depth and reality to your story, but they also help you lead your reader through many triumphs and victories with the characters. Each time your character overcomes something your reader will feel as though they overcame it together and it will bond the reader to your character even more. Furthermore, it stops you from writing an unrealistic story that goes from bad to much worse and then suddenly great again. It provides you with a natural and lifelike flow that allows your reader to feel as though they are genuinely connecting with an individual and not a character that you have made up for the purpose of writing a novel.

Types of Conflict

There are a couple of different types of conflict that exist in every novel. The first one is considered a primary conflict. This is the primary purpose of why you are telling the story, and it is what you will lead up to and wind down from throughout the process of writing the novel. This is the "big one" that will keep your readers engaged and have them feeling like they *need* to know what happens after that particular conflict takes place.

The next type is secondary conflict. This is the type of conflict that takes place leading up to and after the primary conflict. These are smaller conflicts that exist in addition to the primary conflict. For example, maybe in an action-based novel the kidnapper is about to drive a car off of a bridge, so the protagonist has to go save the person who has been kidnapped, but they can't do that until they can get a car because the kidnapper has their car. Here, the kidnapper driving off the bridge would be the primary conflict and the lack of a car would be the secondary conflict. In the grand scheme of the entire story, however, both would be secondary to the greater problem which is that someone has been kidnapped. When you build on the conflict in this way it diversifies everything and adds a more realistic and compelling story base that drives readers forward. Now, they want to know where the protagonist gets the car from if they reach the kidnapper on time, and how they save the person who has been kidnapped. As you can see, it would keep them engaged.

The third type of conflict is an alternate conflict. In a story where third person point of view is used, the author may choose to have two or three primary conflicts going on. For example, for the parents getting divorced might be the primary conflict, for one kid her social life falling apart might be the primary conflict, and for the second kid choosing which parent to live with might be the primary conflict. This story would run with each of these conflicts equally as important as the other, and each one drives part of the story forward until it all reaches an ending whereby everyone is satisfied and happy with the outcome.

When the Conflict Should Occur

Choosing when the conflict should occur in your book is important. There are many different points at which you might desire to put the primary conflict into your plotline. However, it is imperative that you give your reader a reason to care by infusing some form of conflict into the first ten pages.

Some authors choose to start out within' the first ten pages by introducing the primary conflict and then providing the remainder of the wind-down story from there. For example, elaborating further on the plotline where someone is kidnapped, you may write that said person was kidnapped on the first page, or within' the first ten pages. The rest of the book would then be a series of secondary conflicts that result from the primary conflict, until the end where the person is rescued.

Other authors do not want to reveal the primary conflict right away and choose to save it for later. Some prefer to put it somewhere in the middle of the book and provide a fairly even amount of writing leading up to the conflict and winding down from it, whereas others like to put it towards the end of the story and use the winding down process as the opportunity to introduce the "happily ever after" experience.

Where you prefer to put the conflict in your own story heavily depends on how quickly you want your readers to move through the conflict, as well as how you want the conflict to leverage the story overall. If you want it to be the primary focus of the story, you may want to introduce it sooner or at least use secondary conflicts to suggest it starting right away. However, if you want the happily-ever-after story to be the primary focus of the story then you may want to use more casual secondary conflicts to keep the reader engaged while building them up to the conflict and then using the resolution as your final happily-ever-after scene.

Regardless of how you choose to infuse the story with your conflict, one thing remains consistent: you need to give the reader a reason to continue reading your book. Within' the first ten pages your reader needs to understand why they should fall in love with the book through developing relationships with the characters, understanding the importance of the conflicts and how they affect the characters, and what they can expect to feel when reading the book. All of this can be done by how you introduce the conflict, and when.

Questions to Ask Yourself

The following questions are questions you should ask yourself when you are developing your conflict. These questions will ensure that you are clear on what your conflict is and how it affects the story you are telling.

1. What is the primary conflict taking place in my novel?

2. How many primary conflicts do I want involved in my novel? (Note: if you are telling a story from the first person, choose one or two at most.)

3. What type of secondary conflicts can I use to build up to the primary conflict?

4. What secondary conflicts would work well to help me wind down from the conflict?

5. How do I want the conflict to drive my novel forward?

6. When do I want to introduce the conflict and how will that affect the reading experience?

7. Does the conflict make sense to the novel?

8. Does the conflict provide enough reason for the reader to truly care?

9. If I am not introducing my primary conflict right away, what conflict can I use to compel my reader to continue reading?

Chapter 6: Additional Tips

In addition to the basics of writing your novel, there are many additional tips that you can use when it comes to generating a high-quality fiction-based novel that will not only impress yourself but your audience as well. Using these tips when you are writing your story will help you increase the joy you get from the process while also increasing the value of your work. These tips are selected from a series of professional writers and have helped them in the process of generating their own fiction novels. Remember, however, not everyone is the same and therefore you may not require all of these tips when it comes to writing your own novel. Take what feels right for you and your unique story and leave the rest!

As mentioned in the introduction of this book, the tips and information provided within' this book is unique and issued to help you not only create higher quality materials but also enjoy the process. Writing your novel should be an experience that you gain joy from, not one that stresses you out or makes you feel incompetent. If you are struggling, you are not doing it right. The following tips can help take you out of the struggling mode and put you back in the mood to enjoy the experience. When the process is light and enjoyable you will likely find that you produce much better work, so be sure to slow down and readdress your approach if you are struggling to produce the results you desire.

Finally, because of the fact that some of these tips may not apply to the unique book you are writing, you will likely want to keep this information handy for any additional projects you may desire to accomplish. Some of these tips may be more relevant to certain types of books than they are to others, therefore you are likely to find value in new and unique ways each time you return to this book.

Think Outside of the Box

When it comes to writing stories, there are many plotlines that exist that are simply rewritten with different angles and different characters. The setting may be different and some of the events that take place may alter, but ultimately the entire story works out to be similar to several other books within' the same genre. Although the saying "don't try to reinvent the wheel" may ring true in many cases, it is not always the best approach to take when you are attempting to write a new and interesting book that will engage your readers in a powerful way.

Instead of trying to recreate a tired plotline, try thinking outside of the box entirely. Consider the genre you are writing for, such as romance, mystery, or fantasy, and spend some time thinking about parts of the story that are never typically told within' traditional novels from that genre. As you discover new parts of the story that you can emphasize on, make sure that you are truly criticizing them to ensure that there is a good reason as to why this part of the story hasn't been told before. Sometimes a certain element may be rejected or ignored because there simply isn't enough to talk about, other times it may be because that isn't the traditional approach, therefore, most people don't consider it when they are writing a novel in that genre.

Looking at things from a different perspective and discovering new ways to share a story provides your book with a unique twist that allows you to engage your readers not only through incredible work but also through the element of surprise. For example, most romance novels lead up to the part where the lovers fall in love, but what if your novel was more focused on the wind-down? What if the marriage happened within' the first ten pages and from there it was the wind-down and told the next part of the romance story that most novels don't focus on? Paying attention to unique elements of the story gives you the opportunity to still write in your chosen genre while also having the chance to put a unique spin on things and create a story that people weren't expecting.

Ditch Expectations

When it comes to the writing world you will likely stumble on expectations from many different people. Publishers, readers, yourself, other authors, everyone has an expectation of what a book "should" be like. While it is important to consider these elements, especially since some of them can make or break the success of your book, it is also important to ditch the pressure that comes along with them.

Most writers can agree that feeling too much pressure can result in writer's block and it can also drown the enjoyment you gain from writing the book. It can make it feel too much like work and less like an experience to be enjoyed by both you and the readers. Instead of putting that much pressure on yourself, ditch expectations and write for the trashcan. You will likely be surprised at the quality of work you produce when you aren't considering all of the technical aspects of your book.

Set Deadlines

Having deadlines set in place can help you keep motivated, and it can also help you plan for other parts of the book writing process. For example, this can help you decide when you need to begin approaching publishers when work needs to be handed in, when marketing efforts should commence, and more. Having deadlines in place keeps everything moving forward and prevents you from avoiding or neglecting your book altogether.

When you are setting deadlines, however, be generous with yourself. Do not set a deadline that is fixed on a date that requires you to work an obscene amount each day from where you are now until the deadline arrives. Doing this will bring back the pressure and take away the joy of the writing experience. Instead of writing and allowing the story to flow through you, you will be writing under the pressure of knowing that if you don't get a certain amount of words out *right now* that you will officially be late for your deadline and everything will be hindered by your lack of writing speed. Instead, choose a generous deadline that gives you plenty of time to take breaks, step aside and get a breather, and come back to your work to finish it. Be kind to yourself and account for breaks. Most writers do not write an entire book in one straight shot. Instead, they write for several days, or even weeks, and then take breaks off in between to allow for more inspiration to come to them before they carry on. Give yourself the opportunity to have these breaks so that you can take them without feeling pressure.

Get a Good "Test" Reader

When your book is complete, you need to have a good test reader who can read through it for you. This is someone who is not necessarily looking for grammatical errors or otherwise editing your book. Rather, they are simply reading to see if it is engaging and if it will actually appeal to your audience. Naturally, this person should identify with your target audience or their opinion may not count for much.

It is important that you do not hand your book to everyone you know and get as many people as possible. Instead, pick one or *maybe* two test readers who identify with your target audience and allow them to read the book. This way you can get honest opinions without feeling overwhelmed by a number of responses you get. It also helps open your purchasing audience because your friends and family will likely be some of your earliest buyers once your title is launched.

Avoid Perfectionism

Many writers put a pressure on themselves to create the perfect piece of work. They may think of an artist they already know or a series of books they have read that they perceive as perfect and they want their books to be the same quality. Understand that this is not valuable to the writing process and it can actually hold you back from producing high-quality work.

Perfectionism can be intimidating, and it can have you overly critical of the work you are producing. Most of the best books that exist on shelves today were not subjected to perfectionism. Instead, the author focused on telling a great story, not a perfect one. Readers are not expecting a perfect book, they are expecting one that takes them through the story in such a way that is engaging and makes them genuinely feel as though they are present and can relate to what they are reading. Perfectionists need not worry.

Write What You Don't Know

There is a long-standing piece of advice that tells writers to "write what they know", but this isn't always the best way to go. Unless you are deeply passionate about your topic and can infuse it with all of the emotions related to that passion, consider writing what you *don't* know.

Think about a topic that interests you and things you would have to learn based on that new interest. Then, spend time researching it for the purpose of writing the book. For example, if your protagonist is a karate star, consider going to a few karate lessons to get a first-hand idea of what it is like so that you can write from within' the experience. Writing in this way gives you a better opportunity to convey the excitement that you are feeling through your story, thus translating it into the reader's experience.

When we write about what we know, we often don't have the same level of excitement or passion as we would if we were brand new to the knowledge because we have a "been there, done that" feeling towards the topic. Even when we are passionate about it, it can be hard to convey that new childlike wonder through the story. When you are brand new, however, it is brand new to you *and* the reader, and it can enhance the quality of your story through all of the exciting emotions you infuse it with.

Manipulate Your Reader's Emotions

Readers are most often attracted to books that draw out a variety of emotions in them. You want to use your characters and the storyline to manipulate your reader's emotions so that they are emotionally drawn to and attached to the book as you are reading. Many readers agree that the best books are the ones that leave you with a "lost" feeling when you put them down. This is because the reader has developed an emotional attachment to the book, likely based on the writer's technique.

You can manipulate your reader's emotions through a variety of different plot points, experiences, and descriptive phrases. You want to start by helping them become emotionally connected to one or more of the characters, then subject these characters to various experiences that draw out certain emotions in the characters. As a result, it will draw out emotions in your readers as well.

When your reader is emotionally connected to the book, they are far more engaged and much more likely to read it all the way through. Furthermore, they are much more likely to genuinely enjoy the book. Make sure that you play with several different emotions so that the book is not excessively sad, angry, funny, or otherwise. Even if you want to emphasize on one emotion more than the rest, be sure to add a healthy mixture of other emotions so that the book does not become predictable or boring.

Conclusion

Thank you for reading *"How to Write a Novel: Step by Step | Essential Romance Novel, Mystery Novel and Fantasy Novel Writing Tricks Any Writer Can Learn"*!

I hope that this book was able to provide you with many tips and tricks to assist you in the process of writing your very own fiction novel. Whether you are writing a romance novel, a mystery novel, or a fantasy novel, I hope that you were able to learn many valuable methods to increase the enjoyment of the experience and increase the quality of your work overall. This book was designed to help you master the writing process, and I hope that you were able to learn plenty of new and diverse information in order to help you do so.

The next step is to start writing! If you haven't already, begin with your outline and move forward from there. As you are working on your book, be sure to check back with this guidebook regularly to see if there are any tips or tricks related to the part of the process you are presently in. This book was written to be a writing resource that you can check back to as often as you need, so don't hesitate to keep it handy during the entire writing process. You never know what part of the book might become valuable to you during each unique part of the process!

Thank you, and enjoy!

HOW TO WRITE A SCREENPLAY

STEP-BY-STEP

ESSENTIAL SCREENPLAY FORMAT, SCRIPTWRITER AND MODERN SCREENPLAY WRITING TRICKS ANY WRITER CAN LEARN

SANDY MARSH

BOOK 2: HOW TO WRITE A SCREENPLAY

STEP-BY-STEP

Essential Screenplay Format, Scriptwriter and Modern Screenplay Writing Tricks Any Writer Can Learn

Sandy Marsh

reparation, damages, or monetary loss due to the information herein, either directly or indirectly.

Respective authors own all copyrights not held by the publisher.

The information herein is offered for informational purposes solely and is universal as so. The presentation of the information is without a contract or any type of guarantee assurance.

The trademarks that are used are without any consent, and the publication of the trademark is without permission or backing by the trademark owner. All trademarks and brands within this book are for clarifying purposes only and are the owned by the owners themselves, not affiliated with this document.

Table of Contents

Introduction

I want to thank you and congratulate you for purchasing the book *"How to Write a Screenplay: Step-by-Step | Essential Screenplay Format, Scriptwriter and Modern Screenplay Writing Tricks Any Writer Can Learn".*

In this book, you will find all of the information you need to begin writing a screenplay, the details on the specifics of the most common types of screenplays, tips on creating believable characters in your screenplays, how to create a first draft and get to work on editing and tips that have worked for the experts.

You will need the information in this book if you want to create a successful script that will catch the eye of producers to get it to the big screen.

To not develop your ability to write a properly formatted screenplay would be Hollywood murder to your career. Style is everything, and this book covers that.

It's time for you to create an amazing screenplay.

Chapter 1: What is a Screenplay?

A screenplay (also known as a script) is a written output made for a television show, a movie, a video, or a game. When it is written for television, it is also called as teleplay.

Screenplay consists of action and dialogue. Action is where a character is noted to do an action, and a dialogue is where the character is speaking. These two components make up around ninety percent of a screenplay.

What sets a screenplay apart from a stageplay are the use of sluglines. This designates where the scene takes place, and what time of day it is, along with the weather that is occurring at the time. These descriptions are important so that the director can make sure that the scenes are set up properly.

Physical format

Screenplays are printed very specifically. They are also all put together specifically as well. This makes it easier for a producer to get through a bunch at one time. They are generally bound with a cardboard cover and a back page to protect the script when it is handled. Oftentimes, the first copy of the script is the only copy. While it is backed up, it takes a lot of paper to print a script most times, so it is important to save where you can.

In America, the script is usually printed single-spaced on letter size paper. It is printed using 12 point courier font. When it is bound, it is bound using a three-hole punch and held together with two brads. One at the top and one at the bottom. This makes it easier to flip through the script quickly.

Reading copies, those which are distributed, are often printed double-sided to reduce paper waste. This is because there are often more copies that will need to be printed later on, and scripts already take so much paper to print anyway, that finding ways to cut down is a must.

Scripts can often be delivered electronically, but many companies require that a certain amount of copies be handed to the company, or at least mailed if travel is not possible.

Screenplay formats

Screenplays come with a certain set of standards that must be met. These standards are ones that help keep everything uniform and allow for easy reading. They form a sort of blueprint for movies and other screenplays. This also allows a company to distinguish those who take things seriously, from those who have a more laissez-faire attitude. There are software packages out there that can help assist with the formatting of screenplays. This makes it easier to ensure that you will have a professional looking piece to show prospective producers. SmartKey, the first screenwriting software, sent codes to existing word processors. However, the ones today have their own macro entities.

Feature film

If you intend to get a motion picture on the big screen, there are a lot of stipulations for how you have to write your screenplay. The headings, formatting, and spacing all have to meet a specific set of guidelines. While the guidelines may vary from country to country, they are all pretty similar in the fact that they have to be uniform. This is because the rate of transfer from page to screen remains around one minute. This gives a rough estimate of how long the piece will run when taken to the big screen. However, some things often get cut, so it is a very rough estimate.

Nevertheless, if you ever want anybody to not only read what you have written, but to truly take it seriously, you will need to stick to the rules in order to ensure that they have as few obstacles between them and getting to the heart of your story. In general, you can think of the concept of screenplay formatting as mainly an aesthetic choice to ensure that every page of your screenplay is as clear and legible as possible. Each script you turn in should always be written in 12-point, Courier font. This goes for movies or television.

The Slug: Luckily, the Hollywood script format is simple once you learn the basics. Every screenplay is divided into different scenes, each of which represents a different location that the story is viewed from. When a new location is introduced in a screenplay, it needs to be described in a specific way so that the person reading it can automatically picture three key pieces of information. They will need to know whether the scene is taking place inside or outside, the time of day it is and the actual location. Together, these three things form what is known as the slug.

Each scene introduction is going to be written so that it appears on a single line, which will include the location details as well as relevant information about the time of day. The majority of slugs will start with either EXT. or INT., meaning exterior or interior respectively. In general, a slug with start with EXT. or INT. and end with either NIGHT OR DAY unless the specific time of day is crucial to the scene. The only time this will not be the case is during parts of the script where the action is repeatedly cutting between two places or is moving through a number of locations, following a character who starts out from a location that has already been defined. For example: EXT. CAVE – DAY

If you have already introduced the cave in the previous example, then you could simplify by writing BACK TO CAVE.

If a character is moving throughout multiple locations inside a predefined location, such as a house, you can write the intervening slugs as KITCHEN or BEDROOM to maintain the flow of the story while still providing the reader with the details they need.

While not required, the slug often also includes the indicator SUPER which is followed by identifying information and indicates what would be superimposed on the screen for example SUPER: 10 years earlier.

If you are writing a conversation between two individuals who are not speaking to one another directly, you can use the indicator INTERCUT BETWEEN after both of the settings have been determined with a standard slug.

The shot: While the shot will also appear in capital letters with a similar type of formatting, it serves a different function when compared to a slug and shot not be confused with it.

As an example: ANGLE ON JACK, C.U. ON GUN. When writing your screenplay, you will use this technique to draw specific attention to an element of the action. It is typically followed by its own description, almost written as an aside, that is always ended with the indicator BACK TO SCENE before the action from the main scene resumes.

Action elements: An action element is going to come directly after the slug and is preceded by a blank line that runs the length of the page. The action element is responsible for setting the scene, literally, as it describes the setting. In it you will introduce what your characters are doing in the scene that will ideally naturally set the scene for what is going to come next. Any action written in this section should be written in real time, which means you are going to want to write as crisply and cleanly as possible in an effort to convey exactly what the audience will see on screen.

When you write your action elements, it is important to leave out as many extraneous details as possible as this makes the script easier to shoot as fewer unique props will be required. The only time you are going to want to go over the top with atmospheric descriptions is when the atmosphere is crucial to what is taking place on screen. For example, if you picture your favorite horror movie, you can bet that the scene that introduced the main location contain an action element with descriptive text.

However, if you are writing scenes that include lots of tense, back and forth dialogue, or action, then you are going to want to do your best to ensure descriptions are kept to an overall minimum. This will help to create an overall feeling of watching the scene play out in real time which naturally makes your script feel as though it could easily be adapted to the big screen.

In order to write action that plays on the page, the easiest thing to do is picture yourself having coffee with a friend and discussing something interesting you saw on your way to the café. This way you will be sure that you cut out all the filler and only focus on the parts that really matter. During these scenes, you are going to want to keep your paragraphs short, no more than five lines in a paragraph, no matter what. Be sure to capitalize any sound effects that are used. Between each paragraph you are going to want to leave two blank lines. By splitting up your descriptions and your action, you are adding an overall visual emphasis to your story, making it feel more like a movie throughout.

When introducing characters, capitalize the entire name, you are also going to want to include a specific gender as well as age. This information is not only going to be crucial when it comes to understanding what is going on in the story, but when it comes to things like budgeting and casting as well. Make sure you don't go so far as to describe specific hairstyles and clothing, except in situations where it is crucial to the plot. You are also going to want to avoid using parenthesis to indicate action when introducing a character. This means no: BOB (cracks a beer).

When describing movement, you are going to never want to use the word camera. Instead, replace it with the word we. This means no: the camera follows, instead it would be: we follow…

Setting up dialogue: The name of the character who is speaking is going to appear in all caps, tabbed in to almost the center of the page and then directly followed by relevant dialogue. The name of the person speaking can either be the name of the character (BOB) or a description if the person isn't known (MAN IN BLACK). Occupations are also acceptable if they are easily identifiable by the average person. If a character is going to play more than an incidental role in the story they should have a name. Be consistent when you refer to a named character, this means no calling BOB by his name in once scene and then by his last name in the next.

Writing Dialogue: The dialogue itself is going to appear located between the left margin, which is where the slug and the action are written and the margin where the character name is written. Writing good dialogue is certainly an art form all to itself, and most new screenwriters make the mistake of over-writing their dialogue.

The end result of this, in most cases is going to be dialogue that comes off more like a play than a movie, which tends to make scenes seem slower than they might otherwise be. It is important to try and keep your dialogue informal, while at the same time not stuffing it full of as much slang as you can manage. If it is important to the story that you character have a regional dialect, you can mention it when you describe them initially, but do not write out their lines in a regional dialect, unless it is a single line written in such a way to indicate emphasis.

When writing dialogue, it is important to make an effort to reflect the personality of each character in the things that they say, while also walking a fine line of not overdoing it. This will make it easier for the reader to picture the conversation as if it were actually happening, as opposed to two characters in a book, spouting soliloquies at one another. This also relates to the way in which key information is relied by the characters in the scenes. You should aim to express inner feelings in a subtle manner, without resorting to on the nose writing where each character simply says what they are thinking or feeling. Your overall goal should be to make the reader, and thus ultimately the audience, feel as though they are a fly on the wall for a real conversation.

Keep in mind that during almost all conversations, the primary players are rarely going to come right out and say whatever it is they mean. Instead, the conversation is going to have subtext. This means you are going to want to leave out bits and pieces of what exactly is going on and allow the audience the opportunity to figure it out on their own. Not only will this make the scene feel more natural, it will be more interesting to watch (or read) as well. For example, in the movie Jerry Maguire, the character of Jerry Maguire uses the phrase "You complete me" to indicate that he is finally ready to express his feelings for the romantic lead. In this instance, the audience knows he means he loves her because earlier in the movie there was a scene of a deaf couple using sign language and a discussion of the sign for love.

While this example is just a little thing, it still makes the audience think, which is a key to keeping them interested in what is taking place in front of them. As such, you are going to want to consider every line of dialogue that you write and the other possible ways that the same intent could be expressed without directly coming right out and saying it.

Parenthetical information: Any parenthetical information that you need to include in your script is going to appear left indented within brackets, underneath the character name. They are used only to express the emotion the character is currently feeling in the moment. For example, (laughing), (angry), or (upset). Any parenthetical information you provide should always be short, descriptive and to the point. As with any ancillary information, they should only be used when they are crucial to the plot.

Transition elements: Certain transitions are going to be optional, these include things like DISSOLVE TO: or CUT TO:. When you use them, they are going to need to be right indented, not flush right, and should only come after a blank line on the page and should always be followed by two blank lines as well. When you come to the end of page without completing a scene, the scene transition should always stay with the shot that was just completed which means you will never start a new page with either DISSOLVE TO: or CUT TO:, those would remain at the bottom of the previous page.

Transitions are primarily used to denote a major shift in time or location, and sometimes, like using MATCH CUT TO:, for effect. You are generally going to want to leave out transition any time you find yourself rapidly cutting between scenes when adding them in will noticeably disrupt the flow of the sequence in question. This is particularly true for chase or montage scenes.

Chapter 2: Television Screenwriting Considerations

The format for television shows differs depending on how long they are supposed to run. Hour-long dramas are written up much like a movie screenplay, however, there are always breaks for act changes. Meanwhile, sitcoms and other, shorter, television shows are written a little differently which means their scripts have different formats to discern what they are supposed to be. The biggest difference between television and movie screenplays is that the level of standardization between genres, or even varying shows is far less well-defined. There are still going to have some hard and fast rules, however, which means the first thing you are going to want to do before you write a spec script is to read several scripts for the show you are going to be writing for so that you get a feel for what makes it unique.

Nevertheless, there are going to be some similarities in this field as well, and it is important that you understand what they are to ensure you get off on the right foot. One thing that is never going to change is the structure of the show in question. A 30-

minute television show is 22 minutes of content and 8 minutes of advertising (in general) and an hourlong show is typically 45 minutes of content and 15 minutes of commercials. The breaks need to be located in the right spots, which means the act breaks, with two or three additional breaks, depending on the network, for hourlong shows.

Drama

When it comes to writing drama, a good rule of thumb is to start every scene already in progress and make sure to move on to the next too early as opposed to too late. Additionally, you are going to want to be extremely selective when it comes to the scenes you do include, each one will need to either develop your characters or advance your plot, there is little room for anything else. The scenes that are going to end on commercial breaks should end on points of high dramatic tension, even if it is not integral to the plot as a whole. Above all you are going to want to keep your focus on showing, rather than telling.

Common types of dramas: There are several major types of dramas that tend to get produced, this is not to say that nothing else is ever going to get on the air, they are just the evergreen types of shows you can always expect to find somewhere on the dial. The first is the procedural, while this was once largely classified to police shows, there are now countless variations on the traditional solve a mystery in an hour formula, and you can find everything from medical to supernatural procedurals on television these days. The next type is the workplace drama, where there is equal focus on the jobs the characters do as well as on their personal lives.

After the success of *Game of Thrones*, the genre drama went from a small niche to big business. These types of shows typically blend fantasy or science fiction with more grounded characters and interpersonal stories. Finally, there are dramas found on premium cable channels, which can fall into any of the categories, but typically deal in much more extreme content matter and also don't need to worry about the traditional act breaks found in non-premium scripts.

Formatting: When it comes to formatting an hourlong script, if you don't have any sample material to look at, you can safely assume that it will be formatted in the same way a feature script would be, more or less, with the biggest difference being the act breaks. Don't forget, the average page of script is assumed to be about one minute, and the average script tends to come in at no more than 60 pages.

The first page, the cover page, that you provide should include the name of the show above the title of the episode above the writer's name. The next page will be the title name and it should include the same information as the cover page as well as your contact information printed below it.

The average episode is broken up into a teaser, which sets the stage for the episode and is what the viewer will see before the title sequence. The rest of the script will then be broken into four acts. Again, this is only an estimate as there are numerous shows that alter this format in one way or another, the best choice is always going to be tracking down a sample script from the show in question if you hope to be taken seriously.

Each act is going to be given a numerical designation and center at the top of the page that starts the act. Broadly speaking, both Act One and Act 1 are acceptable, just ensure that you are consistent throughout. Likewise, the end of each act should by bookended by End Act _. This should be two lines below the final line of text from the act, bolded and centered. FADE or CUT may be used to end a scene, but this is not required. A simple scene slug will do instead. Each new act should then start fresh at the top of a new page.

The average page breakdown per section works out as follows

Teaser: Between two and four pages

Act one: Between 14 and 15 pages

Act two: Between 14 and 15 pages

Act three: Between 14 and 15 pages

Act four: Between 14 and 15 pages

Tag: Between one and two pages

Total: Between 59 and 66 pages

Narrative structure: Broadly speaking, you are going to want to follow a standard three act structure for your script, the first act should set up the goal for the episode and the end of the first act will generally end with them failing to reach some sort of instant gratification. The second act will further complicate whatever it is that the main character is trying to do, while simultaneously raising the stakes. The end of this act will find the character at their lowest point for the entire episode.

Act three typically begins with something that renews the character's resolve and pushes them to get right to the point where they are going to attempt to overcome their obstacle. Finally, act four resolves everything, though the amount to which this is the case is going to be determined by whether or not the episodes are designed for standalone or serialized viewing.

As a general rule, you can expect the average modern series to include the main plot as well as two subplots that all take place at the same time. The main story is the A plot, the B plot is then the more involved of the two subplots while the C plot, also known as the runner, is typically limited to character building moments. These typically occur about three times throughout the episode. If your subplots are going to be referencing specific details from other plotlines of the television show in question, you will need to indicate where in the series continuity it takes place on the title page.

Sitcoms

The first thing you need to understand about writing situation comedies, is that you already need to be adept at telling jokes in order to succeed in the medium. Specifically, you need to concern yourself with timing as if a joke is executed poorly, especially on the page without a comedic actor to save it, it will fall flat every time.

Multicamera: When considering writing a sitcom script, the first thing you will need to consider is if the show you are considering writing a script for is filmed in the multicamera or single camera mindset. In general, you can expect a multicamera shows to have two acts while single camera shows will more often have three.

The general format for a multicamera show is as follows:

FADE IN: this should always be written in capital letters and underlined.

SCENE the scene should be numbered, capitalized and underlined with two spaces above and below it.

Slug the slug should always be underlined .

(Character list) the character list should be written directly underneath the slug and is used to tell the reader which characters are going to be in the scene. It should be encapsulated inside a parenthesis.

DESCRIPTIONS AND ACTIONS both required actions and relevant descriptions are always capitalized, don't forget to keep these to only plot specific requirements.

CHARACTER INTROS this should always be written in capital letters and underlined.

CAMERA INSTRUCTIONS, SPECIAL EFFFECTS AND SOUND EFFECTS this should always be written in capital letters and underlined.

CHARACTER NAMES AND DIALOUGE these should always be written in capital letters and double spaced.

(PERSONAL DIRECTION) this will appear within lines of dialogue, in all capital letters and enclosed in a parenthesis.

The first page after the cover and title page of average sitcom script will start with the name of the show written in capital letters, exactly six lines down from the top of the page and surrounded by quotation marks. Six lines below this you will want to center ACT ONE followed by A on the next line, which indicates the scene, also centered. 8 lines underneath this you will then write FADE IN: so that it aligns with a 1.4-inch margin. This should be followed by the list of characters that is going to appear in the scene. Each page should be numbered and also include the letter corresponding to the scene in question.

The second scene, and each additional scene will then start on a new page. 21 lines down from the top of the page you will put the scene designation, centered. Six lines below that you will then write the slug. Each act will also begin on a new page. When you are writing dialogue, you are going to want to make it double spaced to ensure it is easy to read. When you write stage direction, ensure you do so in all capital letters in order to more easily distinguish them from the dialogue. Each page should contain plenty of white space to ensure actors have space to write their own notes. In general, the following page breakdown should apply.

Teaser: Between one and two pages

Act one: Between 13 and 20 pages, depending on if the story has two or three acts

Act two: Between 13 and 20 pages, depending on if the story has two or three acts

Act three: Between 0 and 13 pages, depending on if the story has two or three acts

Tag: Between one and three pages

Total: Between 40 and 48 pages

Single camera: Single camera shows are typically going to be formatted more like dramas, though again, specific shows may vary. Even if they have commercial breaks, they may not have a traditional three act structure, especially if the entire season is serialized. When writing dialogue, as well as stage direction, you are going to want to make sure that both are single-spaced. Additionally, each character should have their name written in all capital letters the first time they are introduced onscreen. These scripts are typically the tightest of the three, rarely coming in at more than 32 pages in length.

Additional Tips to Keep In Mind

When writing for a sitcom, above all else you need to nail the tone as well as the voice of each character on the show you are writing a script for. The people who will be reading spec scripts know their shows inside and out and they will respond better to those they can tell know it just as well.

Your spec script should be thought of as your portfolio, resume and calling card all in one. As such, you better make sure it is great if you ever hope to get your foot in the door. In addition to being a tight, well-written story, your script needs to be completely free of all errors, if grammar isn't your strong suit, get someone else to edit your script for you. A lack of concern over the little things won't reflect well overall and could easily be the deciding factor between you and another aspiring screenwriter.

In general, you are going to want to stay away from writing a pilot before you have even landed a job in the industry as pilots from unknowns are rarely picked up. With that being said, however, if you have a great idea for a show, write the pilot episode and then write two or three more. By this point your characters will be more well-established and you can show the reader what your average episode is going to be like. This is crucial as the early episodes of many shows are spent establishing character relationships and interactions, leaving less time for traditional activities and jokes and leading to scripts that seem limp.

Avoid using parentheticals whenever possible. Only leave them in if they clearly enhance the dialogue in a specific way. One of the only acceptable times is when the parenthetical will explain body language that will indicate that the character is saying one thing while clearly meaning something else. Likewise, you are going to want to avoid unnecessary explanations, if you can't make the scene work without explaining it, you should cut it, period. Finally, avoid adding scenes just to fill space, if you can fill out a full-length script with useful content it's time to go back to the drawing board.

Chapter 3: How to Create Characters

When it comes to writing a compelling screenplay, the first thing you that is likely going to come to you is going to be the basic outline of the plot. In order to ensure that this basic idea matures organically into a fully fleshed-out screenplay, the first thing you are going to want to do is more fully consider the characters that are going to be going with you on the adventure you are creating. You will find that getting to know your characters more intimately will make the process of actually connecting the dots on the story much more manageable.

You are not just going to want to only focus on creating a protagonist, you are going to want to consider who are going to be the main characters of your story, both protagonists and antagonists, and write character biographies as well. In fact, this is encouraged, especially if you are writing a feature length screenplay. You want a solid backstory and a solid foundation for writing your character into your story. This is a great way to create a very strong character that will draw the audience's attention until the very end.

Always remember the Theory of Illumination. This theory states that every character reflects on your main character. Their relationships, and their development, eventually lead them to your main character. While giving every character a fully-developed backstory on screen is not recommended, knowing the details of a character's life will make them easier to write for in addition to making them seem more well-rounded as a whole.

This means that you aren't going to want to flesh out all of your character bios in a single evening, you need to spend some time to really think each of your characters through. Take a few days where you spend a few hours to think about your characters, this time should be spent without distractions. No phones, no TV, no music, just you and your thoughts, because you want your character to be authentic, not a copy of a distraction that sticks in your mind. You want a truly original person, not a second-rate copy of someone else's character.

Then, you just start writing. Write anything that you feel is relevant to your character's development. Just let your character grow, and pretty much create themselves, with only the manipulation of the outline you have decided on. This is called free association. Free associating is where you let the words take you wherever, and you merely go along for the ride. This allows you to ensure that your character is not too stiff. You want your character to be real, not forced.

This is not say that everything you write during this period is going to be usable, and indeed much of it may be garbage. However, if you can successfully manage to channel your character for this process you never know what useful information you may end up discovering.

You want to follow every major aspect of your character, true, but you cannot neglect the small things that add up to make your character truly who they are. Remember, people are not made up of only the defining moments in their lives, they are also made up of all of the little, seemingly insignificant moments inbetween. You could possibly do a portion where you outline what their day looks like from the time they wake up, to the time they go to sleep. This will help you better establish the type of person your character will be as well.

If you find an area in your character's life, and you are not sure exactly which way to proceed, let the cards fall where they may. If you are still unsure, do a little research, and go from there. You want to know everything about your character, but you can also be surprised where the words take you. Remember, if you don't like what you come up with you can always scrap it later. When writing your script you should only be focused on creating the best story possible, not with how long the process takes you.

Write! Do not worry about if other people will love it, because if you do not, then no one will. You have to first and foremost be able to stand behind your screenplay one hundred percent. Otherwise, it will not be taken seriously. As the quality of your overall screenplay is going to be dependent on the strength of your characters, it equally stands to reason that you need to love them first, before you worry about anything else.

It is important to create dynamic characters and to keep yourself in line with how you want your screenplay to go. The character has to fall in line with what you want to achieve, and yet they also have to bring a certain element to the table as well. They have to create a little bit of chaos, while also maintaining the peace so to speak.

Imagine you are walking a tightrope. You have to have precision balance. That is what making a character is like. You have to have some flaws as no one wants to root for a character that is perfect. However, too many flaws will make your character seem like a mess, and unless your character is actually a mess, you want them to be relatable. So, you have to walk that tightrope between peace and chaos. This is harder than most people think. As it becomes too easy to make a character extremely flawed, or completely perfect. It becomes too easy to fall to one side or the other, and you have to stay in the middle. It is okay to teeter a few times, but you have to pull your balance back up and continue on.

If you are not able to do so, you will find that the whole story veers out of control, and that can make your screenplay less than desirable. This is what you want to avoid for a plethora of reasons, but the first being that you

Here are my top 5 tips for writing stronger characters into your screenplay:

Make your character likable early on: You have to make your character someone that the audience wants to spend at least ninety minutes with. This means you have to make them likable from the get-go. Even if you think the character is interesting, if they are not very positive, or they are annoying, the audience will lose interest before you get to the good parts of the character.

You want the audience to be able to identify with the character because that is what draws their interest in. The main character should be written as the protagonist, this way the main person is not a self-serving, negative drawback to the screenplay, unless the entire purpose of the screenplay is to chronicle their downfall or their redemption. In general, however, people want to see the negative characters portrayed as the antagonist. This way there is some balance between good and bad though, typically, good will win out in the end.

Your character does not have to be perfect, they just have to have some redeeming qualities. These qualities will help your character reach out to the audience in a way that keeps them interested. You can do this by making the dialogue witty and conversational. You can make them do a kind act in the beginning, such as saving a cat from a tree. In fact, there is an entire screenwriting book, entitled *Save the Cat* for just that reason. Regardless of the setup you choose, you just have to make sure that you set the tone for a likable character early on in the story. This is important, because if you do not, you may find that you lose your audience's interest before even grabbing a hold of it properly.

If you have a character that maybe does not have the best qualities, then it is important to include other, worse, characters to make him seem better in comparison. For example, if you have a character that may be in prison, you want to make him better than the other prisoners. Your character does not have to be a saint, just better than the others, and more relatable than a villain. They have to have a sense of purpose about them, to attract the audience to the plot line, and help them retain their interest until the very end. A complex character cannot get lost in his flaws.

Build realistic & detailed characters: While the character is who your person is, characterization is what they are. One is the true deep soul of the character, the other is the shallower, facade that they present to the rest of the world. For example, you could have a lonely woman who just wants someone to love as a character, but her characterization could be a CEO of a company who acts like she does not need anything from anyone. This is characterization. Sometimes the two are similar, and sometimes they are polar opposites. Like a hard, edgy teen is truly a softy on the inside. These contrasts, when revealed, make for a more detailed, believable characters, and a better storyline. People love to be surprised and love finding out more about the characters in a story. So, you have to make sure that you detail their characterization precisely. You want to make sure that you put

some emphasis on who they are, but also what they are as well –
the inside and the outside.

Writing strong characterization is important on so many
levels. First off, a realistically depicted character will add a lot of
realism to your piece. I cannot count how many times I've seen
the same generic antagonist in a film that had zero original
characterization, which ultimately completely diminished their
importance in the film. But even outside of just adding realism to
the characters, it can also help you as a writer to tell your story
more intuitively and dramatically.

Just like you want to write a character biography, you also
want to create characterization sheets. These help you discern
what your character will be like throughout most of the
screenplay. You can do this quickly, through another round of
free association. Give your character choices, as if they were
living, breathing, individuals. It is important for you to be free
flowing with your characters so that they feel authentic and
realistic. If you try to force your character to completely match
someone who inspires you, the character will feel forced. Let the
character speak to you. Which, coincidentally, brings us directly
up to the next tip.

Let your character make the decisions for you: Many writers feel that their screenplay has to be completely mapped out before they even begin writing, and while it is important for you to make sure that you have the structure outlined, it is equally important to let your characters breathe, otherwise the setting will feel fake and forced, which is the opposite of what you want.

Rather than forcing your character into a box that you have neatly outlined before you have even touched the first sentence, you should let your character make their own decisions. This may sound silly because you are the writer, but the truth is, once you have spent enough time with your characters this will seem much more reasonable. Once you have spent enough time chronicling their likes and dislikes, you will find that you will be able to easily picture what they would do when confronted with a specific decision. You want them to come alive and come off the page, which means you have to let the characters take control sometimes. This allows the scene to feel more realistic, and give it more depth.

While your character may be an extension of yourself, they are also a separate entity from you as well and should be treated as such. With that being said, however, if you give a character a trait that you share with them, then it becomes much easier to anticipate how they would act in a given situation as you can use your own experiences as a point of reference.

If you have already created a character biography and a characterization sheet, then this should be an easy thing to do. You should know your character inside out, and as your character grows, how they will make their way through the story should become clear. So, while you might have thought the character could go one way, you may be surprised when you get to that point, and find that another solution suddenly makes more sense.

Likewise, you are going to want your characters to grow organically which means letting them change as the story dictates, as opposed to forcing them to remain in a predetermined box. Not only will this do a disservice to the character overall, it is unsatisfying for an audience to leave a character exactly where they started, either mentally, emotionally or physically, unless that fact is central to the overall plot. You want them to be like real people, because they will be portrayed by real people, and your target audience will be real people, so you have to make sure that your character has depth.

Approach the early drafts with an open mind, and that will help you build an organic, relatable character. Even if it means you have to change a lot because one choice changes everything.

You will find that the more you let your character choose, the more realistic the story will feel, and the more interest the story will garner. This is what you are looking for because you want the character to draw the audience in. It is important that you write some serious choices in as well, as a screenplay without real consequences is likely lacking in dramatic tension as well.

Give your character compelling dialogue: Dialogue was touched on earlier, but it is important enough to warrant further consideration. All of your characters need to have a strong dialogue. This will establish who they are within their first few lines. Even if they do not have a lot of lines, the ones that they have should be solid, and discerning.

So much can be conveyed by the simple use of dialogue. Accent can determine where the character is from. Their sentence structure can determine how educated they are. The tone of voice can determine if they are introverted or extroverted. All of this and more can be shown just by how the character's lines are written.

Something as simple as a scene where a character is running errands, and talking to the people they meet can tell a lot about the character. This may seem odd, but it is true because they are showing a piece of themselves in their everyday life.

Even though the narrative films are fiction, people want them to seem as realistic as they possibly can. This is because people like what they can relate to. They want to be able to feel a connection to a character, even if it is an animated character. Dialogue is a great way to do that.

Compelling dialogue is not always a lot of dialogue. You could have a character that speaks very little, and yet they could be a very dynamic character. How you set up their dialogue really sets the tone for how they are portrayed. You have to make sure that no matter how many lines of dialogue a character has, they are set up to portray a depth to that character.

Something that you want to stay away from is one-dimensional dialogue. This is where all of your characters speak the same. Even if they are all from the same area and same family, every person speaks differently. While similar characters may have similar dialogue, they should also have their own unique characteristics in their dialogue. This will help you discern the different people when the storyline starts speeding up. If you have all the same dialogue, the characters will blend into one another.

#5 – Think like an actor and give your character a point of view

One of the most important things to think about is the character's point of view. As the writer, you see everything, but the main character does not. You have to make sure that you are writing with the character's point of view to ensure that confusion does not set in by the character knowing something that would be impossible for them to know. This clutters things up and makes it hard to keep the scenes straight.

If you are laughing at this tip, you need it the most. You cannot just slap a character down all willy-nilly, you have to put some thought into it. You want a character that will be easy to figure out so that the actor can do the character the justice they deserve.

The most important reason to write a strong point of view is that it gives a line for the story to follow. The audience needs to understand where the character stands, and if the character does not have a solid point of view, then this gets harder to do, and it gets frustrating for the audience, the actors, and everyone involved in the creation of the work you have worked so hard on.

Have you ever seen *Forrest Gump?* In the movie, the main character, Forrest Gump, has a very strong point of view. In fact, the entire movie is told from his point of view. You can see where he stands on life, love, and running. This is what you are looking for in a character, even if it is not written in first person point of view.

There are so many screenplays that lack this concept. These are the ones that often get tossed out because no one wants to be confused for ninety minutes. They want to be able to easily follow the character.

Some scenes are drawn out longer than necessary because the character does not have a strong point of view, which causes the scenes to run around in circles. This makes it harder to follow, and more confusing for the audiences that you may have.

A test to see if you are heading in the right direction is to see if you could cut the scene down to no more than two pages. While some scenes need a lot of dialogue, there are still ways to cut it down to make those two pages, and if you cannot do that, then perhaps you have to reevaluate the scene and the character's strength in their point of view. It is best to do this in the editing stages to see what needs to be changed.

What else can we do?

There is no set formula for how to write a character, but if you follow these tips, you will be off to a good start. It is important that you find what works for you because you have to have a solid character for your storyline to move forward.

In fact, all of your characters need to be strong, so that they move the story along smoothly. A bad character is like a speed bump. It interrupts a steady pace and can be frustrating if there is a lot of them.

There are other tips that you can find from other writers as well. Spend some time with your local writer's guild, or go to the library. This will help you immensely to find yourself and find the character you are looking to create. You have to have a solid grasp on your character, for them to flourish.

Go out in the world, and people watch. You can get some ideas for character traits you would like to have in a character. Walmart, the mall, the park. These are all great places to find interesting characters.

Chapter 4: Creating a Rough Draft

Most contracts that you enter into will give you three months maximum from the pitch to come up with a rough draft. Three months may seem like a good amount of time, but it is actually not a lot of time. You have to work swiftly, and efficiently to get your rough draft out in time. Otherwise, you may lose your shot.

Something that helps is to remember that screenplays are time-related. While a novel can be as long or as short as you would like, most feature films run between ninety minutes and two hours. This makes it harder, and easier at the same time. It gives you an idea of how many pages to write but also makes it that much more restrictive to write with a deadline, and a page limit as well. You want to make sure that you streamline the process, to make things go a lot easier.

Getting a good workflow will give you a good storyline. You do not want to seem like you rushed the development. Here are some ideas for a good workflow.

Develop the story idea:

Before you can come up with a story, you must first start with an idea. You cannot just slap words on a page and call it a screenplay. Go somewhere that inspires you, and get an idea for the story from start to finish.

Create the pitch:

Then you have to create the pitch that will give you an idea of how the story will flow. Start with the five finger pitch. This is where you list some major events on one hand. These events once explained should flow nicely. If they do not go do some more thinking. If they do, then you can move on to the two-handed pitch which is just more events that flow smoothly. Once this is complete, you have a solid foundation for your storyline.

Give it structure:

This is like adding the walls to a house. You have to add more turning points, and supporting events. You want to be able to hold the story up, and by giving it structure, then you can have a full blown story coming your way soon.

The importance of structure is that it keeps the entire story from just falling apart at the seams. If you do not have a strong structure of your house, it will fall down. Same with a story.

Build a full story:

Also known as a synopsis, this is where you get all of the major events mapped out. Basically, the synopsis is a one page summary of the entire story. It is the story without all of the minor details and dialogue. Once this is done, you can move onto the next step, which brings you closer to actually writing the rough draft.

Create a beat sheet:

This is a basic outline that will help you keep track of where the story is at, and where it will go next. The outline does not need to be really detailed, it is just a little bullet point list that you can check off as you pass each point in your writing once you finally get to writing your script.

The importance of a beat sheet is to ensure that you are keeping up with the storyline, and moving at the proper pace. Otherwise, you will find that you are stuck, and being stuck can cost you precious time.

Write the script (finally):

Woohoo! It is finally time to get to script writing. You have to make sure that your outline is complete first, and then you can get down to business. There are a lot of software out there that will help you, as they already have the formatting ready for you. Some also have tips and tricks for writing a good script as well. If you are not sure of your abilities, there are software out there that will proofread your script as well for you, though they are a little more costly.

As you are writing, you may find that you need to tweak what you had previously written. Do not go deleting anything yet, instead, create a list of things that need to be fixed, and when you go to edit your rough draft afterward, then you can create an edited rough draft later on. This way you can keep things on track, and get your first rough draft punched out.

Do not delete your original rough draft. It should be kept as your first draft in case you need to go back and reference changes. Once you have edited all of the additional things into your script, you can celebrate.

NEXT STEPS:

The next step is to get your rough draft to the company you have a contract with. They will look it over, and tell you if they like it, and what they feel needs work. Then you can get to editing.

Chapter 5: Editing a Screenplay

Have you ever wondered why a character is rarely seen eating, drinking water, or going to the bathroom unless it has significance to the storyline? The reason these things are rarely portrayed is that this would be too much information, and would drag the story on too long.

In any storytelling form, you have to edit the life of a character in some way. This will keep the storyline moving, and keep it from getting tedious. Bathroom breaks, minor incidences, and repetitive action are generally not important in a storyline, so if you have too much of these, they should be edited out.

Before a screenplay is produced, there are many ways a writer can edit their screenplays. Whether it be through editing and rearranging scenes, juxtaposition, and cutting the fat. All of these are resources that will help the editing process move forward.

Juxtaposition is important to use in any form of art, and screenwriting does not escape its grasp. Just by changing the juxtaposition of scenes, you can give the story an entirely different feel.

This can be used in one scene or two scenes, or depending on how many you need to use it on to help get the point across.

Crosscut and parallel action are two points of juxtaposition that are most commonly used in writing, and they are found to be very effective in creating different tones for different scenes, which is what writers want to achieve.

For instance, a very fun moment cut directly into a boring moment can accentuate that boredom through contrast.

Juxtaposition is a word that is not overlooked in any editing class. It is useful in so many areas, from writing to cinematography, and stage preparation. Prop work as well. The contrast it creates can be useful in setting a tone and creating a mood. This makes it less necessary for words to set the tone, which will leave you more words for important things.

Sometimes, you get so attached to your story that you do not want to cut anything, but the unnecessary parts are important to cut because they just slow the production down. It is important to cut them before they get to production if possible because you do not want to waste more time than you absolutely have to.

Some directors are more spontaneous though. They want you to leave it all in, and they will see how it works as it is being filmed. However, if you cannot get a scene to work when you are writing it, it is still best to leave it out.

However, if you are lower budget, you should make all of the necessary cuts before production, because any delays can cost a lot of money. If you do not have that much money, to begin with, then you will have a hard time recovering.

Removing weaker scenes do not just help production, they help the budget as well. Every page of the script costs money, and if you cut the weaker scenes that wouldn't make the cut anyway, then you save the money it would take to produce them.

Cutting scenes post-production also causes a lot of problems with continuity in a piece as well, because there is not enough time to smooth out the edges.

The continuity of a film is really important. Without that continuity, it will feel like someone gave a twelve-year-old a camera and told them to make a movie.

It is important to take the lighting into consideration as well. Consider how the light will affect the mood. So when editing, you have to pay close attention to the lighting to make sure it stays consistent. Fix it if you need to because the wrong lighting could set the wrong mood, which would shut your whole production down. If you do not want that you will make sure to specify the time of day in every scene.

Not only does the light change, but your character may also change as well. If a lot of time progresses, your character cannot stay the same the entire time. You have to make sure that you have made note of the changes as the film progresses.

The visuals are usually clear-cut, but if scenes need to be cut in post-production, that can disrupt the visuals. If several scenes need cut, then you may find that certain scenes need to be reshot to fix the visuals. This is another reason to focus on editing closely.

When editing, it is important to keep in mind the order of the scenes to ensure that the continuity is there. If something needs to be switched around, make sure to adjust it accordingly, so that the visuals are smooth, and there are no visual speed bumps when you hit production. Because it becomes a lot harder to fix on the spot then, and you want a smooth transition to have a successful film. Visuals are very important, and it is important to remember that.

Another part of editing is to make sure that you note the transitions. Every film has to have transitions between scenes so that they flow smoothly. Otherwise, you would have to add a whole lot more information. These transitions are a lot easier to add in the editing process than the post-production days. So make sure to make a note of the transitions before it becomes harder to add them.

Another reason to make sure everything is solid in editing is that there can be unwanted interpretations if you have to cut scenes in post-production. Doing so between similar scenes can create confusion, and doing so between contrasting scenes can be jarring and dramatic. This can be used to say something if it is intentional. However, if it is not intentional, you risk saying something to the audience that you never meant to say, which can leave them confused.

Also, directors do not like to be told how to do their job, so avoid technical directions in your script. Instead be subtle in telling the director where the camera should be pointed. Instead of saying "Point camera to the west." You could say "The main character looked off into a beautiful sunset, contemplating the meaning of life. Since the sun sets in the west, the camera will point west.

Editing can save you from a lot of issues later on in life and ensures smoother transitions as you head into production. It is important to make sure you edit out all of the kinks to save money when it comes time to shoot the film. Now if only taxes could be edited out of our lives.

Chapter 6: Tips for Success

While there are a wide variety of reasons that you might want to be a screenwriter, if you are hoping to do so in order to adopt a shorter, less stressful, work week you may be extremely disappointed. In fact, successful screenwriters are often extremely disciplined, dedicated individuals who have trained themselves to create something from nothing, day end and day out in order to ensure they always have something productive in the pipeline. While what works out to be an effective process for each writer is going to differ, sometimes dramatically, the most successful all typically have a number of habits in common that make the task before them more manageable. These are outlined here, in hopes that at least a few of them will inspire you to write more successfully in the future.

They have a reason to write: The best screenplays, especially those written by first time screenwriters are written with a specific purpose in mind, by writers with a driving desire to tell a specific story. This doesn't mean that your motivations for telling your story need to be pure as the driven snow, after all, entertaining others is as good of reason as any. The important thing is that you have a reason that is strong enough to drive you to continue trying to tell your story no matter how hard the going is going to get, and it is likely to be quite difficult from time to time.

Regardless of the motives that you have for writing, you need to be passionate about it if you ever hope to find true success. Don't feel ashamed if part of the reason that you want to write a successful screenplay has something to do with egotism, remember, the goal isn't to make yourself want to write a screenplay that will change the world, it is to find what drives you to write, and in this case egotism is as useful of a reason as any. Everyone wants recognition to some degree, and if you want to write for revenge, glory, fame, money, power, or simply to prove that you can, then you can harness that energy and use to make you a better writer, ensuring you actually see the screenplay through in the process.

They demand the best from themselves: When you first start writing your screenplay, it is perfectly acceptable to leave in placeholder scenes and text, from time to time, just to ensure you make it through to the end in one piece. With that being said, it is important to keep in mind that the spec script your produce is going to be the one, and often only, thing that people in the industry look at when they decide if they are going to give you your big break which means that settling for anything less that absolute perfection is akin to throwing away all the time that you ultimately spend on your screenplay.

As such, it is important to never settle with your first draft, your second or even your fourth. You are going to want to go through the entire thing with a fine-tooth comb until the story is as tight and compelling as possible. While this is only going to ever take you so far, it will at least ensure that the screenplay that you send in is the most accurate indication of what you are capable of as possible.

At the same time, you are going to want to make a conscious effort to stop making changes at the point where the work, as presented, speaks for itself as you can always find something to tweak or change. Eventually you are going to need to have the confidence in yourself to put the work out there and, hopefully, start receiving feedback on it. If you don't practice restraint, your screenplay will likely end up feeling overwrought, as you will have overthought whatever spark was there to begin with into oblivion.

They write what they like, and what they know: While anyone can have an idea for any type of story, and that story might be unique, or relatable, enough to resonate with the world at large, you will typically find that it is much easier to write about things that you have first-hand knowledge about and also much easier to keep at it if you like whatever it is that you are writing. Again, it is perfectly acceptable to get into the screenwriting business for its potential for lucrative gains, this in no way means that you can't enjoy the process along the way. What's more, if you find the story in your screenplay exciting, the odds are high that those around you are going to feel the same way.

Likewise, when it comes to writing what you know, this doesn't mean writing a movie about being an accountant for an accounting firm, unless you have an idea that will make the process seem roughly 2,000 percent more exciting than the topic naturally seems to the average person. Rather, adding in touches from your every day life can make certain characters more believable, or giving one of your hobbies to a character can make them seem more three-dimensional. What's more, you never know when something from, even a seemingly boring job, can provide you with the one realistic, but unexpected, fact that you need to tie the whole plot together.

They set goals: If you have never before found yourself sitting in front of a blank screen, with all the freedom in the world in front of you, only to find yourself looking for any excuse to be anywhere else, then the idea of setting writing goals to ensure you actually finish your screenplay may seem unnecessary. The first time you make the decision to bolt rather than face down your writer's block, however, you will realize just how vital setting goals can be. Likewise, if you have never written anything substantial before, then you may find yourself doing all the research you need to complete your screenplay, only to find that you never actually get any closer to generating a truly finished product.

As such, you should start by setting goals for your pre-writing process, including generating characters, a basic plot synopsis, world building elements etc. You should give yourself plenty of time for the more free-form nature of this part of the process, though you should have a firm deadline when you want to begin the actual writing to ensure that fleshing out your characters doesn't end up taking years to finish.

When it comes to writing the first draft, you are going to want to make a concentrated effort to write for at least an hour a day, at least five days a week, and also spend some time on the sixth day coming up with a general idea of where the end of the next week should find you. Writing every day will help to ensure that you don't lose the flow of the story as it can be hard to recapture lost momentum once it has slipped away. While writing for a set period of time is fine, you will find that you will be more productive still if you task yourself with writing a set number of pages each day. This will ensure that you maintain your productivity, rather than just waiting out the clock on days where inspiration takes longer to strike. In addition to page goals, you are going to want to have a general idea of where you want to the story to go next, so you can steer things in that direction.

When it comes to editing, you are going to want to set hourly goals, as it is difficult to say just how much work you will get done per session as it is going to vary so dramatically. When it comes to setting an overall timeline for completion, you are going to want to give yourself enough time to ensure you don't rush, but not so much that you don't feel obligated to make daily progress. When setting these goals, it is important to keep in mind that they are not taking place in a vacuum. Writing for three or four hours every day is an admirable goal, and likely one that is completely unrealistic if you already have a fulltime job. It is important to set goals that are achievable as failing to do so can harm your morale and making finishing your screenplay harder than it already is.

Finally, the overall length of your timeline isn't important, as there is no standard amount of time it should take to create a quality screenplay. The most important thing overall, is that setting a schedule will help you to make finishing your screenplay a priority which means you are going to be far more likely to finish it than you otherwise would. Remember, your screenplay could be your shot at the bigtime, but the only way you will ever know for sure is if you actually finish it.

Conclusion

Hopefully, you learned a lot about writing a screenplay from this book. It was filled with plenty of tips on how to proceed. This is important because you cannot just jump in.

Now, you can go out, and start working on your screenplay. This book can be your guide if you whenever get stuck.

Thank you and good luck!

More by Sandy Marsh

Discover all books from the Writing Best Seller Series by Sandy Marsh at:

bit.ly/sandy-marsh

Book 1: *How to Write a Novel*

Book 2: *Outlining*

Book 3: *Story Structure*

Book 4: *Plotting*

Book 5: *Character Development*

Book 6: *How to Write a Screenplay*

Themed book bundles available at discounted prices:

bit.ly/sandy-marsh